FAUNS & FAIRIES

the adult fantasy coloring book

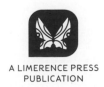

A LIMERENCE PRESS
PUBLICATION

FAUNS &
FAIRI

the adult f
coloring bo

& IES

tasy

By Trungles

designed by *Hilary Thompson*
edited by *Ari Yarwood*

PUBLISHED BY LIMERENCE PRESS
Limerence Press is an imprint of Oni Press, Inc.

Joe Nozemack, publisher
James Lucas Jones, editor in chief
Brad Rooks, director of operations
David Dissanayake, director of sales
Rachel Reed, publicity manager
Melissa Meszaros MacFadyen, marketing assistant
Troy Look, director of design & production
Hilary Thompson, graphic designer
Kate Z. Stone, junior graphic designer
Angie Dobson, digital prepress technician
Ari Yarwood, managing editor
Charlie Chu, senior editor
Robin Herrera, editor
Alissa Sallah, administrative assistant
Jung Lee, logistics associate

Trungles.com
twitter.com/Trungles

LimerencePress.com
twitter.com/limerencepress
Limerencepress.tumblr.com

First edition: September 2017
ISBN: 978-1-62010-403-3

PRINTED IN HONG KONG.

1 2 3 4 5 6 7 8 9 10

THIS BOOK BELONGS TO:

_____

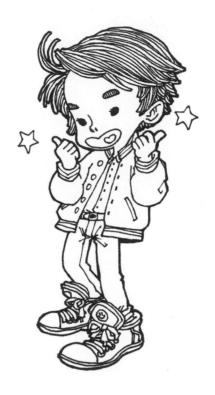

TRUNGLES is a comic artist living and working in Minnesota. He specializes in fairy stories and fantastical narrative works, borrowing heavily from early 20th century illustrations for children's stories, parochial texts, and ephemera. His foray into pornographic content might be considered something of a hard left.

READ MORE LIMERENCE PRESS BOOKS!

OH JOY SEX TOY, VOL 1
By Erika Moen and Matthew Nolan
ISBN 978-1-62010-362-3

OH JOY SEX TOY, VOL 2
By Erika Moen and Matthew Nolan
ISBN 978-1-62010-363-0

OH JOY SEX TOY, VOL 3
By Erika Moen and Matthew Nolan
ISBN 978-1-62010-361-6

OH JOY SEX TOY, VOL 4
By Erika Moen and Matthew Nolan
ISBN 978-1-62010-444-6

OH JOY SEX TOY: THE COLORING BOOK
By Erika Moen and Matthew Nolan
ISBN 978-1-62010-376-0

SMALL FAVORS: THE DEFINITIVE GIRLY PORNO COLLECTION
By Colleen Coover
ISBN 978-1-62010-398-2

LIMERENCE

For more information on these and other fine
Limerence Press comic books and graphic novels visit
www.limerencepress.com. To find a comic specialty
store in your area visit www.comicshops.us.